Everything Worth Fighting For:
An Exploration of Black Life in America

Copyright © 2016 by Chris "Dasan Ahanu" Massenburg
All rights reserved. Published in the United States of America.
Second edition.

No part of this book may be reproduced or transmitted in any form, or by any means, electronic or mechanical, including photocopying, recording or by any information storage or retrieval system without written permission from the publisher.

Everything Worth Fighting For
2nd edition
ISBN (Trade pbk.)
978-1-7330502-9-6
Layout and Design: Chris Massenburg
Cover Art: Gemynii Evolving
www.piecesofagem.com

HPJ Writeeasy Publishing
Durham, NC

www.dasanahanu.com

For Omisade.
Thank you for your wisdom, strength, and vision. You have been an anchor and guiding light for so long. I appreciate you being willing to share your brilliance in this book.

For Gemynii.
Thank you for being a roaring flame of strength and will. I've watched you claim your voice and show the world your magic. It is an honor to be in your corner.

For Ajamu and Rukiyah.
Thank you for raising the revolutionary I aim to be. Thank you for introducing me to the cadre of warriors that have shaped the way I see the world. Thank you for blazing a trail. Thank you for the belief and love.

For Bryan.
Thank you for taking me in. Thank you for pushing and challenging me. Thank you for constantly reminding me what glorious fight looks like. Thank you for allowing me the space to become.

Thank you to M.D. Marcus
Your keen eye was very helpful. I am honored to have such a talented writer to talk poetics with.

Table of Contents

Preface	i
Foreword – Omisade Burney	xi
Modern Fruit by Gemynii	xvii
To Be an ARTivist by Gemynii	xviii
Introduction	xx
Grandfather's Parable	1
Lula	3
Amore Noir	8
If I Had A Son	12
Dear Daughter	15
Litany for Tomorrow	19
Requiem for Change	22
Burn	28
Simple Complexities	32
Miracle Whip: A Villainous Villanelle	36
Wilted Flowers	37
Body Language	40
Blues for Midnight	43
Sciaphobia	47
Safe	50
Spike Lee	54
Everything Worth Fighting For	58

Preface

When I first decided to take my poems into an open mic venue and conquer my stage fright, I went in with a rising social consciousness. In my mind, I was Dap freshly awoken from ignorant slumber at Mission College (*School Daze*). In reality, I was somewhere between a Chris Rock and Eddie Griffith stand-up routine. I was just coming home from spending time at NC A&T State University (spending time is the best way to describe my academic progress there) where I had a number of different consciousness raising experiences.

In the two amazing years I spent in Greensboro, NC taking classes at that fine institution, I had attended a presentation by Steve Cokeley, spoke with brothers from the Nation of Islam, sat with students of Malachi Z York, broken bread with militants, been challenged by nationalists, and been introduced to various revolutionary principles and readings. Yet, I didn't have any context into how this impacted action. I had lots of anecdotes and inspiration, but no experience. That would soon change. As I began to become more involved in the Raleigh arts scene, I came to meet activists who were not only versed in revolutionary principles, but were active on their campus or in the community. The sarcasm and bohemian cynicism was being replaced by a new understanding.

While meeting activists who were similar in age and similar in passion for change I was also introduced to elder freedom fighters in the area. They saw the potential in us and took time from their fights to help us find our own place in social justice work. I was invited out to different programs and trainings. There they celebrated our youthful exuberance, inspired us to learn more, and they pushed us to get involved. I did. Soon I was learning to put principles into action.

Over those next few years I dedicated myself to learning how to grow as an artist. At the same time I was also learning about what activism really meant and how to organize. The paths were framed as parallel. I wanted them to become intersecting, but the worlds still remained very separate. That bothered me.

Guided by wonderful mentors and inspired by amazing peers, I had the opportunity to help plan major actions and demonstrations, start radical organizations, lead workshops with organizers from across the country, be on organizational steering committees, hold a position in national leadership, and collaborate with a variety of groups. Still, I felt that what I was becoming as an artist was not being wholly integrated into what I was doing as an activist and an organizer. Don't get me wrong, my art was heavily influenced by it. My politics guide my creative work. The issue was the fragmentation of my skills and abilities. The art community wanted one thing. The social justice community wanted another.

I was at a crossroads. I decided that I wanted to dedicate my time differently. The arts took priority and most of my organizing energy. My activism stayed intact, but I decided to apply what I had learned to mobilize a different set of cadre.

In addition to continuing my creative development I decided to become an arts organizer. My aim has been to try to build community as artists (especially Black artists and other artists of color working in what would be considered urban contemporary arts), to bring art to the community, and to create art that the community could be proud of. I wanted to do this while figuring out how to make change, inspire change, or plant visions of change as an artist. I wanted to help connect artists across boundaries and to create greater capacity for more art through newly woven networks. I also wanted to try and create a model of development that integrated attention to craft, a belief in the necessity and responsibility of self-determination, awareness of space and place, and a social justice framework.

Since I first began my journey I have had a variety of experiences that have shaped me forever. Those experiences, the people I have had the honor of meeting and working with, and the wonderful cadre of dreamers and fighters I have learned from and fought beside lead me to where I am today. I work in honor of everything poured into me that helped me to develop my identity as an artist and helped me to discover my voice in this world.

So I tell stories. Stories from the margins, stories of self, and stories of those who will one day topple buildings with the indomitable will they are learning to harness. I put pen to paper and create. Rhymes, plays, articles, poems, love notes...I write from a place that feels like those who helped learn me are watching just over my shoulder. I write with responsibility and accountability. I write with southern charm, feminist politics, and desire to never stop dreaming.

I also try to build capacity. I develop programs, coordinate events, schedule meetings, consult projects, teach classes, facilitate workshops, create new outlets, secure venues, and dance to muzak whenever possible. I support, encourage, mentor, advise, and brainstorm with artists. I remember watching a video of Amiri Baraka talking to Askia Toure about the Black Arts Movement. They discussed how their focus was not just to create art, but also to build institution. I think I was a craftsman in another life.

I create and I build. That drive has led me to develop a project called Radical Voice and Artistic Expression (RVAE). In these times, I think this project very necessary.

What do I mean by "radical voice"? Let's look at the dictionary definitions of both.

Radical - of or going to the root or origin; fundamental: favoring drastic political, economic, or social reforms: forming a basis or foundation: existing inherently in a thing or person.

Voice - something likened to speech as conveying impressions to the mind: expression in spoken or written words, or by other means: the distinctive manner of expression.

How we see the world guides us. It is our vision that defines our mission. It is our perception that shapes our reality. Influencing how people see the world is an important factor in impacting change. Art can affect how people see the world. We have an amazing power as artists. We have the ability to capture the attention of those who agree and disagree for however long our artistic presentation takes. In that moment we are given great latitude. In that moment we are opportunity.

We need "radical voice" in contemporary art. This isn't a new concept. In the 20th century alone we saw it with the Harlem Renaissance, the Beat Movement, and Black Arts Movement. We need to continue the tradition and adapt it to our changing world. That means a multimedia and multi-genre artistic response.

Think about this quote from the 1932 Manifesto developed in NY by artists, members of the John Reed Clubs (US journalist who covered the Russian Revolution):

"We call upon all honest intellectuals, all honest writers and artists, to abandon decisively the treacherous illusions that art can exist for art's sake, or that the artist can remain remote from the historic conflicts in which all men must take sides. We call upon them to break with bourgeois ideas which seek to conceal the violence and fraud, the corruption and decay of capitalist society."

Now look also at this quote from the "Manifesto for an Independent Revolutionary Art" by Andre Breton and Leon Trotsky (signed by Breton and Diego Rivera). The manifesto can be found in Breton's *Free Rein* published by the University of Nebraska Press:

"True art, which is not content to play variations on ready-made models but rather insists on expressing the inner needs of man and of mankind in its time –true art is unable not to be revolutionary, not to aspire to a complete and radical reconstruction of society. This it must do, were it only to deliver intellectual creation from the chains which bind it, and to allow all mankind to raise itself to those heights which only isolated geniuses have achieved in the past."

That is why RVAE brings artists together to discuss how to integrate their artistic and their creative talents (vision, innovation, analysis, etc.) into movement building and social change. There are organizations doing amazing work in communities across the country. They need hands on deck to forward that work. They need to reach new hearts and minds to build the movement. They need partners in strategy, framing, and propaganda.

That's where artists come in. They can help add to the national narrative. They can provide counter narratives to dominant rhetoric. They can help spread the word of work that is happening. They can tell stories of those at center (targeted) and in the margins (devalued, overlooked, or ostracized). They can be a living archive of radical thought. Every major social movement in recent history has been chronicled in art & culture. The goal is for art and its creators to become more than an accent at an action. Cultural workers/creatives should be a part of the strategy. Not just a momentary hype, but a sustained inspiration and agitation.

Artists can also help activists and organizers build movements. Their way of thinking can help inform the process. By bringing their creative abilities into the meetings, artists can help shape the scope of the actions.

RVAE believes that new possibilities for arts activism can be sparked once artists are able to have discussions, envision collaboration, shared thoughts and ideas, deepen theory, and connect.

In RVAE, Radical Voice is defined as a distinctive manner of expression aimed at the root or origin of an issue; favoring drastic political, economic, or social change; and conveying revolutionary and redemptive principles inherent in radical social movements.

The concept is inspired by a business principle outlined by Albert O. Hirschman in *Exit, Voice, and Loyalty* that identifies "exit" and "voice" as strategies for expressing dissatisfaction with an entity. "Exit" is quitting use or association or switching to a competitor. "Voice" is to agitate and exert influence for change "from within."

So Radical Voice is a multi-genre artistic agitation intended to exert influence and inspire change.

Social movements have become the catalysts for change in our society. Art is reflective of social movements. As Thomas Reed notes in *The art of protest: culture and activism from the civil rights movement to the streets of Seattle*, these movements have shaped our politics, our culture, and our political structure as much as any other single force. People identify a problem, determine that responsible parties are failing to address it adequately, and therefore take action, themselves.

Social movements happen when groups of individuals or organizations work towards or in opposition to change on specific political or social issues. In *The Peyote Religion Among the Navaho*, cultural anthropologist David F. Aberle identified four kinds of social movements, which are alternative, redemptive, reformative, and revolutionary. In this typology, redemptive (individual level) and revolutionary/transformative (group level) models seek radical change.

RVAE recognizes that art communities/scenes share many of the characteristics of social movements (including their rhetoric). Within these communities/scenes there is art that we as artists know has had and continues to have redemptive and revolutionary/transformative impact. So imagine what can happen when that art is integrated into movements that are focused on bringing about redemptive and revolutionary change.

RVAE is an opportunity for artists to get in a room and talk radical voice, arts and activism, and how to lend their art to the movement. RVAE is part workshop, part discussion, and part peer skill and strategy building session. RVAE sessions are guided by a facilitator, but are led by the collective energy, spirit, and passion of the participants.

Maybe I like to gather cool people together in a room. Maybe I need a way to make new friends. Maybe I don't want to feel like the only outlier.

Maybe I believe art can help us survive, help us sustain, help us win.

I developed this project and shaped it into three foundational workshops that are intended to build radical arts collectives in communities. I crafted the theoretical framework and then piloted in my community. I then marveled at the collective genius and wisdom of the artists who showed up.

Those amazing folks let me know that I am moving in the right direction.

This book is how I plan to introduce the notion of this project to the world, or whoever gets this book. As I worked on pulling this project together and conducting the sessions, I was inspired to look critically at the world around and at myself. That led to me putting pen to paper. It always does.

The book idea really came together when a fellow artist asked me what did I feel compelled to do with my art in this moment. Amidst the headlines, protests, lost lives, hashtags, social media debates, and ongoing frustration at the obstacles to living a full and fruitful life I found these poems.

I offer them to you with a heart hopeful that they will inspire. I offer them as a declaration of the work I am dedicated to doing.

Let's make this place beautiful.

Foreword

ex·plo·ra·tion
/ˌeksplə'rāSH(ə)n/
noun
the action of traveling in or through an unfamiliar area in order to learn about it.

African American explorer Matthew Henson was born in 1866 in Maryland, one year after the Civil War ended. He left home at 13 and became part of a ship crew. After a few years, he arrived in Washington, DC where he would meet the explorer Robert Peary at 21 and became his "First Man". He was an expert craftsman, dogsledder, navigator and fluent in Inuit. He is the first person, along with his Inuit guides to reach the North Pole in 1909, 111 years ago. Lt. Commander Nyota Uhura was born star date 2233, 368 years after the civil and was the top communications commander of the starship USS Enterprise under Captain James T. Kirk. She was of African descent, spoke fluent Swahili, and was a mathematical and communication genius. Her first name, Nyota, means "star" in Swahili and her last name, Uhura, is a derivation of "Uhuru" which means "freedom". It was her job to manage and maintain all communications between the members of The Federation as well be the first point of contact with new species encountered during space exploration.

Like Mansa Musa, Esteban, Jean Baptiste Pointe du Sable and Mae Jamison, they set out into landscapes and realities that were unknown to them. They stepped into spaces that requires intellectual and cultural curiosity, attention to detail, multifaceted skill sets, leadership, the ability to be a strong and flexible teammate, tenacity and humility. It is in the exploration of the unknown that new worlds emerge that changes the way you see yourself, the world and the place you call home. The journeys taken, lessons learned, failures and unimagined discoveries, requires meticulous documentation for those coming behind. Things like "don't eat this--for it will surely kill you" to the appropriate culture deference and respect to be shown to foster diplomatic ties and not mortal enemies are critical. However, It is in the exploration of who you are---the reimaging what we think we know about Blackness and dropping down deeper into our own identity that real magic and healing happens.

My parent's room in Maryland during the 1970s always smelled like a mix of Charlie perfume, Old Spice aftershave, Captain Black tobacco and Jergen's lotion growing up. Home was my first place to explore my Blackness. The costume jewelry, afro wigs, dashikis, shoe trees, a jar of quarters that was not to be touched for the ice cream man and Mary Kay cosmetics were open to terrain for my sister and I. We touched, smelled, tried on everything we could find quietly and meticulously as we explored every bit of their room. In that exploration we learned that our mother's middle name was Ella from old identification in the bed side table drawer. We also figured out that my daddy was a 33rd degree mason and that while the bible sat on the dresser, Playboy and Hustler lived in the back of the closet in a box. We were our own mini archeologists meets museum docent, sharing what we found with each other, taking each other by the hand to dig deeper into the nooks of places not seen to further bear witness to who our parents were besides our parents.

Their Blackness, as I reflect on it now, was drenched in southerness that had taken a new, but familiar shape in an urban setting. It looked like house parties with Curtis Mayfield and Donny Hathaway bedtime lullabies. Croakers, fried hard, Old Bay steamed crabs and Johnny Walker Red. Saturday afternoon Soul Train and Sunday morning James Cleveland. It was all around us to breath in, taste, touch and explore. That's who we became too.

somebody/ anybody
sing a black girl's song
bring her out
to know herself
to know you
but sing her rhythms
carin/ struggle/ hard times
sing her song of life
she's been dead so long
closed in silence so long
she doesn't know the sound
of her own voice
her infinite beauty
she's half-notes scattered
without rhythm/ no tune
sing her sighs
sing the song of her possibilities
sing a righteous gospel
let her be born
let her be born
& handled warmly.

---Ntzoke Shange

I was 20 years old in 1987 and a student at UNC Chapel Hill. It was the year that I enrolled in Dr. D. Soyini Madison's Performance Studies of African American Literature course. It was during the course, that Dr. Madison, revealed to my classmates and I that the Black authors whose names we knew from our book learnin' were actually oracles to our Blackness. I have spoken publicly about my experience with her and silently thanked Dr. Madison a thousand times for blowing my mind at 20. She was the original driver of the magic school bus and she fearlessly and graciously took our class by the hand to personally pulled us through the portals created by the oracles to introduce us to Janie and Tea Cake, Maude Martha, Sula, Luther Needed, Sassafrass, Cyrpess and Indigo. She conjured the great griots of a generation into the room and we broke bread and had tea with Alice, Gloria, Ntozake, James, Maya, Nikki, Toni and Gwendolyn. The role Dr. Madison played was dynamic and complex. She teacher, midwife, conjurer, seer, sensei, and guide. She was aperture. She also spied our own evolving stories through her looking glass and created a protective portal for our voices to come through brilliantly, clumsily, but always authentically. We time traveled down to the deep south, uptown to Harlem, across the seas and back landing in the amen corner. Words, stories, prose, and poetry were our blueprint. The imprint from this experience over 30 years ago is still revealing itself to me as I learn and unlearn who I am as a Southern Black woman.

In the Ifa Yoruba cosmology, the supreme deity is called Oludumare which translates to "owner of." It is said in one of the Ifa origin pataki's (myth or legend) that when Olodumare finished fashioning the universe, they said "Ase, it is done" to which they heard a voice respond "who said that?". That voice is said to be that of Esu, the Orisa of the crossroads, the master communicator, the Orisa who is personified as the gatekeeper and arbiter of mankind. We are reminded of our free will through Esu's presence and that all of our choices of "this or that" result in consequences or blessings that are about alignment with our heavenly destiny. Esu has been characterized as a trickster because of their perceived mercurial nature. All rituals begin and end with Esu as they are the owner of the many paths that takes our prayers to heaven. I like to think that this origin story reminds us that time is not finite and that what we assume is a beginning or an ending is actually an iteration or loop. This loop gives us another opportunity to lean into the possibility that before our consciousness, something else existed that informs that moment of our birth.

I met Dasan the summer of 2004 when my eldest son Che was a participant in a community documentary camp at the Center for Documentary Studies at Duke University. When I heard Dasan read his poetry, I knew that he too held the keys to these spaces of exploration. I knew that he had time traveled and I could see the words that tumbled out of his mouth take the form of a spyglass into our many truths. The beauty of it all…joy, sadness, pain, regeneration and love. As Black people in this country, it feels like we are on a constant quest of exploration to find the "true" beginning of our origin story. Our various points of origin can sometimes feel like a cold case file until we tap into tools or technology that reveals that the deeper parts of our individual and collective experiences are iterative.

We have been gifted with the ancient technology of stories that acts as cultural currency. The words of the stories told vibrate at a frequency that unlocks portals that exist inside of each of us. The words illuminate, reveal maps and infinite truths about what it means to be Black that is expansive. Dasan knows this technology, he has studied that code. He has followed the path left by those explorers and oracles who came before him, carved his own way and has taken the hands of those who would arrive later and pulled them through. We are invited to view his documented journey and see, feel, and smell the places of intersection of our collective stories that allows him to quantum leap into and through black holes. This book is a snapshot of his travel log. It is an offering, a prayer, an incantation and spell. This book of words, his words invite us to come along and remember who we are, again. Explorers.

Modern Fruit

By Gemynii

Strange fruit no longer swings from southern trees
They walk down streets in hoodies
while being hunted
They drive cars stopped by overseeing officers
They sleep on their grandmother's sofa and never
wake up
Strange fruit bears seeds they sometimes
never see fully bloom
Yes they bloom through concrete streets
Still stained with yesterday's blood
Strange fruit prays
Sometimes too quick to forgive
They yell for help
They run
Strange fruit sings
They resist
Strange fruit becomes hashtags and names on signs
They record themselves being cut down and tossed
aside
And the world continues to consume them

To Be an ARTivist

By Gemynii

Being both an artist and an activist means I am what you would call an "ARTivist." I discovered my love for painting and my need be a part of the reemerging of revolution in this country both in my mid-twenties. My passion for art came first and it was all about expression. It was my release of emotions that words could never fully capture. Initially it became a tool for rebellion for me against standardized beauty and for me to tell the story of what was going on in my world as a queer black woman.

I rebelled against what I saw in the fine art world and media with images of larger bodies, images that explore gender and sexuality, and black culture. The work I have created over the years was never merely for only entertainment or pleasure. I wanted to produce pieces that challenged oppression and that encouraged audiences to more critically think about the stories, the beauty, and experiences of people of color. My paintings and my acts of activism both reflected my deep interests in exploring issues around cultural and racial identity, definitions of beauty and sexuality, history, justice, community, freedom, and love.

My journey into activism began as a reaction to the increasing state of awareness of a nationwide problem with police brutality and the continued lack of respect for black and brown lives. I was angry at a society that continued to protect and defend racist cops. I felt deep sadness for the parents of children whose lives were cut short due to ignorance. I was tired of existing in a world that loves black culture but has no real love for black people. And I wanted to have a more active role in doing something about it.

I found myself marching and protesting in rallies concerning matters in my world such as the treatment of the LGBTQ communities and Black Live Matters. But I wanted to be more than just a participant in rallies and demonstrations. I felt that as an artist, my ability to create needed to be my contribution to the movement by presenting images audiences needed to see. A thought that is very similar to radical black female artists who came before me such as Nina Simone. "You can't help it. An artist's duty, as far as I'm concerned, is to reflect the times."

In combining my love of art and my passion for justice, I knew that art alone will never be enough to change the way society views people of color in this country. The creation of art won't be enough to put a complete end to all of the social and political injustices that continue to plague communities of color.

Art has never begun or ended wars. But it does play a heavy role in the evolution of our culture. It has the power to start conversations. It can lead to potential connections in a movement aiming to uplift, change, and heal communities. And being an Artivist means I have an active role in making that happen.

Introduction

I have had a very overactive imagination since I was a child. It is that incessant sense of wonder that made the Black folk around me spectacular characters full of flavor and amazing. In the people I got to be around I found more fuel than I needed to keep the wheels turning for hours on end. There was evidence of the amazing at my Nanny's (mother's mother) church, in the rides out to the country with Grandpa Joe, at the grocery store with my mom, in the moments spent trying not to overhear my aunt's conversations, and while sitting on the floor of the living room as my paternal Grandmother gave her impression of most things to whomever came to visit. Black Life was a magnificent thing to me.

I grew up with this perspective. Always a watcher, I found great joy in letting my mind race with possibilities as I examined the people around me. I loved to observe, overhear, pick up on, and discover. Nothing was more interesting than Black Life. Maybe I was just transferring my love for fantasy and mystery to my surroundings. I was a kid who became engrossed by all 10 volumes of L Ron Hubbard's *Mission Earth*. My favorite texts to date are the books of Sherlock Holmes by Sir Arthur Conan Doyle. I was a huge fan of Agatha Christie's Hercule Poirot stories. Growing up in a working class family I consumed a variety of used books. To this day I don't remember where they all came from. I was just happy to have them. My mother was happy I was reading so voraciously. Many of them weren't filled with Black characters. I didn't mind. I found those in real life.

Even though I saw amazing in the Black folks around me, it took me a while to find my own. I was raised on good manners and appropriate behavior. I was also raised a southern gentleman. I have never forgotten my aunt making sure I understood to open the door for a woman, wait to sit at the table, walk on the outside of the street, and other facets of proper gentlemanly etiquette. I obliged in order to avoid a hand smack, shirt tug, or side eye. I respected my elders. I said, "yes sir or yes ma'am" in response. I tried to stand as straight as my mother preferred. I was considered smart, articulate, and mannerable. I was shy before I knew what introverted was. I was chameleon before I knew how to code switch. I was silent before I heard of marginalization. I was a "good" boy and consistently complimented on how I acted and performed. It was ok. I developed a skill that allowed me greater access to watch and dissect. I was uncovering my magic. How to be, in all the various ways you can be anything, and not be all while soaking in every aspect I could.

Curiosity and discovery was a gift and a curse. It made me love learning. It also made me adore mischief. It made me never doubt Black amazing. No matter what was going on in the world. No matter what headline captured everyone's attention. It helped me through depression. It taught me resilience and the ability to adapt. It led me to sit with, listen to, converse with, and learn from militants, freedom fighters, nationalists, socialists, communists, five percenters, members of the Nation of Islam, and street corner wisdoms who knew more downs than ups. It pushed my understanding of Black amazing further than I would have ever predicted.

It wasn't long before I knew I had to tell these stories. I just had to. I was Black and southern and I wanted the world to know how much that could mean. But it didn't stop there. There was a deafening breath of Black stories that needed to be told from all over this country. It is these stories that are always close to the tip of my pen and along the face of my keyboard. I want to make these Black folks and their amazing tangible in people's minds.

"For, while the tale of how we suffer, and how we are delighted, and how we may triumph is never new, it always must be heard. There isn't any other tale to tell, it's the only light we've got in all this darkness." – James Baldwin "Sunny's Blues"

There is the wisdom, courage, and strength of our elders that we must celebrate. Sometimes it is Grandpa or Big Mama or the stern but loving woman we learn to reference with "Miss" in the front of her first name. Sometimes it is a mentor we find at just the right moment or the voice that sees what we couldn't and articulates it to us when we least expected. Maybe it is the woman whose ability to show us how to love unconditionally leads us to respond by filling in the space made empty by the devil's untimely work. We have to talk about it. We have to recognize that they are what overcoming looks like. They are our living blueprints.

At the same time we look to our past and the foundation it provided, we also have to consider our future. Our children are some of the greatest offerings we can give to this world. It is this growing hope that we try to nurture and protect. They are our sons and our daughters, our nieces and nephews, our cousins, mentees, players, or students. They remind us why we survive the night to face another day. Palms pressed together preface wishes for their success. They also accompany tears and angst over promise gone too soon. We know they should survive.

There is magic in our own experiences. Lessons learned and insight gained. It is our responsibility to share that with others. We have to tell what we know. We have to act like we know. It may mean standing alone. It may mean facing the unsettling of every bit of comfort we have established. We have to understand that sometimes interruption can be glorious freedom.

Think about all that we have face and still face in this country. We continue to push on fully aware that regardless of the achievements, the strides, and the resilience there are still those who will never see the amazing for what it is. Yet here we are. Here we will be. Still magic.

We know that we cannot rest. We must struggle on. We must keep each other aware. This is a complex life we live. Dubois taught us of duality. Today we are learning of layers, peeling away the rhetoric and exposing a harrowing truth.

But we are amazing, magical even. So we take this truth and craft new horizons, shooting stars, and daydreams. Songs sung, instruments played, canvases painted, stories told, and poems written.

We do this with one reminder that we want to sear into the minds of all who engage our art.

We are everything worth fighting for.

"A dreamer is one who can only find his way by moonlight, and his punishment is that he sees the dawn before the rest of the world." – Oscar Wilde

Grandfather's Parable

Let me tell you something bout getting by boy
See God breathes life
and we all carry Holy Spirit like helium
See we're all just balloons
Strung to existence on earth
but desperate for the heavens

But be careful now boy
Because the devil is watching
Ready to capture wishes like fireflies
Bottle them up in self-doubt and fear
I say let's protect them
Exhale them into stretched possibilities
Tie them up with your grandmother's memory
and send them skyward
Like balloons

They'll be captured by angels
given wings before puberty
Skipping through playgrounds dressed in white
Singing destiny and holding wishes
Blinding the devil with their smiles
So make sure they're your deepest
Because those tickle the most

Like mama's hands by surprise
when she whispers "I Love You Baby"
and kisses you on your forehead
Filling you with happiness
like air in balloons

Boy
You take your fears and hesitations
Take your stress and worry
Your pain and heartache
Take your desires and wants
Take your revelations and insights
Fill your hope with them
Tie them up with faith and let them go
like balloons
But remember, the devil is watching

Lula

Ooh, that's why I'm easy
I'm easy like Sunday morning
That's why I'm easy
I'm easy like Sunday morning

She pranced like pixies amongst the forest
after evil was cast out by an unexpected hero
Bellowed from somewhere happiness
holds authoritative positions
You know,
where joy is in charge
I watched it
every Saturday morning
As Miss Lula swept her front porch singing
Singing like a Wednesday night at the Apollo
Friday night at the Cotton Club
Saturday at the juke joint
My mother just laughed at Miss Lula
Hoped for the same spirit at that age
My father called her crazy
I called her amazing
Then called for a singing lesson every Saturday
because learning how to let go
was always followed by candy and pop
She would tell me
Dance like no one's watching
Sing so God can hear
Smile like you don't remember how not to
Miss Lula was inspiration, a survivor
Outlived conflicts, racism, Reaganism
Tie-dyed tees, unfair sentencing,
black power fist picks,
her husband and two sons

Miss Lula knew about struggle
The struggle watching cancer steal
the other half of your soul
All while glued to that hospital chair where
she planted her hope until it wilted
The struggle watching a misguided plane
stealing your legacy
Stuck to that rocking chair
with eyes glued to the news
She hasn't smoked since Earl passed
Cooks sweet potato pie every September 11th
because it was the boy's favorite
and won't go anywhere she can't be driven to
She's sung her song every Saturday
With her favorite backup dancer
shuffling all the dust she swept back where it was
She swept and I danced
We spent the morning entertaining absent souls
that we knew were smiling in admiration
Because the sun never shined brighter
It didn't rain on Saturday for 6 months
Sun asking for encores
I've never seen her smile more
as we moved from the porch
to the living room

I remember the day I first saw the pictures
Full color portraitures of Lula's solitary frame
I wondered why they had replaced
the pictures of her family
I had assumed it was to reduce the ache
of missed moments
She told me that absence
isn't a lack of presence,

it's a loss of imagination
She made me look again
Curated my insight into faith's art
I looked at Miss Lula
standing alone under an oak
with a wide-eyed look of surprise on her face
She said that's Earl and me
under our favorite tree
His lips on my cheek reminding me
that this is where we had our first kiss
I looked at a picture of her alone
on a blanket by the lake
That's the boys and me out there fishing
She said
they never caught more
than each other's understanding
Lula continued
Explaining the unexpected reality
of each recent snapshot
See her family never left
Just left behind our expectation
for their existence
This woman was an anomaly

How do you look at beds not made
since her candies were devoured by hatred
Her boys misguided and martyred
It's said that chocolate melts in your mouth
and not in your hand
Her son's promise melting amidst
burning fuel lit by conspiracy
and ate up by a disparaged public
How do you walk past bedroom shoes
at the foot of an easy chair
it's so hard to imagine empty

See Lula made those beds every Saturday
only for them to need to be made again
Straightened that easy chair
only for it to be spread out in comfort
in front of the TV every Friday night
Picked up men's clothes off the floor
Tossed them into the washer
only for them to be sprawled out
across the bedroom floor again
Was this a mystery
or the answer to moving on?
Never let your memories move out
I opened the refrigerator
Saw a case of Miller Lite
6 bottles missing
I thought that this might be the inspiration
for Miss Lula's perseverance
Then walked over to the sink
and smelled the residue
of disbelief poured daily down the drain

They say doing the same thing over and over
expecting a different result
is insanity
See Lula found peace in madness
Because no one wants to take
a crazy woman's last dream
She told me that she knows
they think she has lost her mind
They just lost their hope
Too quick to toss their faith aside
Boy…don't you ever let them
take away your magic wand
Cast your imagination
wherever you damn well please

Remember
The only time you ask for forgiveness
is on your knees

The first Saturday it rained
was the day Lula stopped singing
Now she resides with her husband and sons
I haven't lost my imagination
Now I cast my spells on a page
Tell you to read between the lines
Let me curate your insight into faith's art
Let me paint pictures with words
My ideas and thoughts aren't alone there
Pages filled with the stories of people like Lula
Filled with stories of every angel
who found their halos dimmed
by the shadows of burden
I pour my heart into these poems
like Miller Lite down drains
So you can smell the residue
of southern elder wisdom
I still sing every Saturday morning
Sweeping my eyes of the illusions
this world gives
I'm still dancing like no one is watching
I can do this because Lula showed me the way
So I turn up the volume
and let the music play

Ooh, that's why I'm easy
I'm easy like Sunday morning
That's why I'm easy
I'm easy like Sunday morning

Amore Noir

Sister I love you

I love you like dusk loves sunsets
When anticipation sets over my shoulder
for your touch when you arrive
I love you the way midnight loves moonlight
Because in the darkness of your eyes
I find the stars that plot my happiness
I love you like gardeners love manure
Because you're the only one who can
put up with my crap and
still make this relationship grow

I love you like
February loves the 14

Like forgotten slaves loved Juneteenth
I love you like I love my best friend
I love you to completion
like the beginning loves the end

I love you like dry hair loves split ends
Because when our love runs dry
splitting up is the only way we can begin again
I love you like bedtime loves prayers
Because on my knees is the only way
I can give God thanks for lying next to you
I love you the way fingers love sending text messages
Because the instantaneous response
of your skin to my touch
is the reason I love to have sex with you
I love you like magnets love refrigerators

Because the attraction of your intelligence and
determination is why I can't help
but be next to you

I love you like my heart
loves its beat
Like summer days
love the 100-degree heat

I love you like arrested development loved speech,
hoping you can Dionne Farris my insecurities away
and your melody of wisdom can fill in where
I have nothing to say
I love you like kool-aid loves sugar
Sweet like the kisses you give to me
I love you like Granddaddy loves a grill
So, I flip these words across these lines on this page
like some ribs hoping that you savor every
love poem I have to give

I love you like white sand
loves Carolina blue beaches

I bite into the fruit of your labor and find what
commitment tastes like
So, I love you like the juice down your lips
from some country grown peaches

Like nature loves
the four seasons

Like revolutionaries love freedom

I don't know why I love you,
but it's a damn good reason

I just love you

I love you like drunks love cheap liquor
At the bar taking shots of naughty head (Seagram's 7)
I run my fingers through your scalp
to find the root of why you're so special
Places kisses on your cheek
taking shots of your knotty head

I love you like peanut butter loves jelly
I preserved the hope I would meet someone like you
Now I find your buttery brown skin
between those white sheets like two pieces
of white bread
I spread myself across you and
bite into insatiable

I love you like po' folks love tax returns
I have been taxed in every relationship that wasn't you
So I file this 1040 hoping that it's EZ
for you to return the prayers I have given to God
that I would find someone like you

I love you like heathens love Saturday night
at the licka house and still make it to
Sunday morning church service
Because when I look into your eyes
tear stained and glassed over
any potential indiscretions have me guilty and nervous
I love you like babies love mommy's breast
because you fill me with emotions
that sustain my being
I love you like we take for granted
the blessing of seeing
Like blind people love daydreams

and I never appreciate you fully
until your no longer in my sight
I love you the way the wind loves a kite
because your words have my spirit flying high
so, a conversation with you is how I want to begin
every morning and end every night

I love you
like I love myself
I love you like
I love no one else
I love you like

A newborn loves its first breath

Like a body loves death when there's no breath left
Like it would feel like death if I had no you left

And since there's no poem left, then with this last breath…
I say…
that I love you

If I had a Son

Baseball caps, sneakers, and guilt
Tainted bloodlines and travel schedules
Prayer and therapy
If I had a son
I'd tattoo his name on the inside of my wrist
So each rubbed forehead
reminds me why I push

My blade of a boy
In sharp contrast
to the butter knife belief
that I would never bear this burden
What better way to slit
Drip these blues
Make myself think I can ink restitution

If I had a son
He'd be a moonshine melody
A sweet potato pie promise
Homemade, strong, intoxicating
Have me leaned over for kisses
Stumbling at the thought I made that
Mix of sugar, spice, and everything nice
bout his mama's love
Baked in her belly
and pulled out the oven southern
Sweet

If I had a son
I'd study astrology
so I could understand the wonder in his eyes
I'd bury treasure in the dimples in his cheeks
for his mother to find when she kisses him

Dear boy
Your daddy is a farm of a man
worked over season to season
for the crop he grows from his lips
Goated into caring
Milked of his compassion
Henpecked over chickenshits
Mule headed
Thank God your mama was a tractor of a woman
Your Nana a well of wisdom
Your Granpa a scarecrow in a field of wheat and barley
They helped make this work
But you will not be hard soil to till
if I can help it
I will dream you city skyline

If I have a son
I'll read him books by sunlight
We will listen to Jazz and Hip Hop by moonlight
So that when dawn comes
he will have proper insight to guide him
But when night falls
he will follow the groove inside him

I will let him know that his mama
was a front porch rocking chair,
War and Peace with lemonade and biscotti,
WOMAN
A Coltrane sampled and looped,
sweat and whiskey,
looking for the perfect beat,
shell toe and bamboo earring,
Cannonball Adderley and DJ Premier,
WOMAN

Teach him he will know his own completion
when his daydream looks him in his eyes
and answers the question
he never asked anyone before

If I have a son
He will be the liquor my daddy never let go of
The joy I see in my momma's eyes
The prince at a table of advisors
Uncles with arsenal of double entendre
Ain't scared to shoot it straight
1 phone call
They show up
1 phone call
The police show up

Son
There is so much to tell
So much to share
So far to go
So much to see
So many minutes spent
Making you better than me
But always remember
I couldn't have made you without your momma
We both know she was heaven sent
So imagine what God intends you to be

Dear Daughter

You are the better than
I always wished for
The smarter than
the mistakes I've made
The most beautiful gift
I could ever inherit
The most amazing poem
I could be inspired to write

I was given care of a book
Bound with resilience and faith
Covered in dawn's horizon
Name etched with the tip
of God's fingernail
Nicole
The copyright page
doesn't include my name
But the chapters bear my touch
and I aim to help
make the ending wonderful

With the turn of each page
I marvel at the woman you
are becoming
My first instinct is to protect you
To save that open heart
from loving the wrong person
To save that bright spirit
from being tainted by disappointment
To make sure a father
is never the absent conversation
you have to have with God
He gave you me

and I plan to honor that opportunity
with pride
and unrelenting care

I know this world
The ills it holds
The wonders it possesses
I know you are destined
to make it bow at your feet
There is a destiny
written in the heavens for you
I see it when I look in your eyes
My job is to usher you there
To teach you that each setback
is preparation
That each break through is a benchmark
That each obstacle
is affirmation of your ability
to rise to the occasion
Mountains become molehills
Because next to the blossoming
will inside you
Those peaks pale in comparison
This is what growth is about

I didn't make you
but I raised you
Job not quite complete
But it is probably the most
rewarding one I have ever had
To hear you call me
Dad
To hear about the life you live
The life you want
The hope you hold

The strength you bear
The wisdom you haven't fully
learned to wield
But it's there
A combination of your
mother's prayers,
nana's wishes,
and the redemption
of the man that helped create you

There isn't anything I won't do
to maintain that smile on your face
Nothing I won't do to preserve
the flame in your soul
There is an unforgiving jury
out there
But they can't render a verdict
that can determine your future
No judgment
from narrow minded ignorance
can convict you less than you are
Your life is yours
Never forget that
You beauty is unmistakable
They can't take that
They will learn the wonder you are
or marvel from a distance
But I will make sure to remind you
that they matter not to the
walk God has in store

This book
that tells an Angel's tale
is the best in the library
I relish the writing of each chapter

The etchings
are a wondrous reminder
of the blessing of parenthood
I don't know how I ever
proved worthy
But thank the Lord
he saw fit to allow me the chance
What a glorious irony
That the writer
finds inspiration
in helping you craft
the next page
In helping you take the next step
in your journey

My darling daughter
You
are the tears welled in my eyes
The joy in my laugh
The concern in my brow
The one I know will
make tomorrow
bellow your name in reverie
Thank you
for allowing me
along for the ride

Litany for Tomorrow
(Inspired by Audre Lorde's "Litany for Survival")

There are those of us with kissed foreheads
and our parents hopes in our smiles
who may soon disappear
We are the children you call blessed
Carrying promises made with hands clasped
and head lowered in prayer
We sit in classrooms blending daydreams
with short attention spans and inspiration
We make memories between the dawn's sun
and the night's moon
Seek a tomorrow
we too often find
snatched
by blind justice
Become martyrs
instead of miracles
But this nightmare doesn't reflect the dreams
we hold

There are those of us
who prefer optimism over fear
Who wish with enthusiasm
and love like play will be forever
We don't want to see demons in mirrors
or familiar hate in the midst of eyes
This is an illusion of well-placed headlines
and prejudice
The foolish refuse to see the value
in all of us
The brilliance and fire and innocence
We were intended to survive

We are the doctors who might not ever
find the cure
The lawyer who may never get to challenge
that statute
The chef who will not get rave reviews for the
genius in the menu
The writer whose best seller may be the t-shirt
with screen printed memorial
We are the actors who won't see the standing ovation
on opening night
The teachers who won't inspire the next to know
they can become now
The mechanic, the storeowner, the designer all
vanishing in the midst of gun smoke
Athlete or Entertainer, Politician or Revolutionary
games never played
songs never heard
speeches never given
We are everything the future should be
if they weren't afraid
of us getting there

We are the laughter God can't hold back
that causes leaves to fall in autumn
We are the choir of caged birds covered in
the ink of Auntie Maya's pen
We are the lighthouse eyes that guide you to
work and back everyday
to provide us a better way
We are the hugs that feel like the wings of
guardian angels
The kisses that become timely affirmation,
well placed and well received
We are whatever the heavens destined us to be
We are the breakthrough waiting to happen,

the lost waiting to return, the wild and rambunctious
waiting to be calmed, the star waiting to shine,
the diamond in the rough waiting to be found
We are everything you know we are
and nothing the media would make you believe
So it is better to fight for us, teach us, mentor us,
love us, raise us, discipline us, listen to us
knowing
that we were intended to survive

Requiem for Change
(For Survivors)

The words don't always
seem adequate enough
off my tongue

I'm still choking back tears
after all this time
I guess it's learning
you can never be good guy oblivious
for too long
You can't be enough royalty
to not need to keep challenging
yourself
Ain't no ribbons for books read
and chivalry
This here is a long road traveled

The first shared tears came in high school
She was trying to reconcile what happened
I was trying to use balled fists in revenge
She was telling me she didn't want that
I never realized I was making her
manage him and me
It took too long to recognize her strength
Good guy said you should have stayed with me
Good guy said let me fix it
Good guy still made it about good guy
I guess I felt
I couldn't make it about her because
I wasn't good at tears falling

Daddy liked liquor and women
Liked to swing heavy hands

I never asked to know about
anything else
But I know the dangers of that recipe
Good guy wanted to redeem
him by being the first
good decision he ever made
Wasn't I the one who had to go
pick up his pride
from houses he was no longer
wanted in?
Good guys learn to fix things early

Good guy asks stranger if he
can walk her to her car
Never wonders why she might refuse
Might get mad at the answer
He be good guy
Good guy ask questions for understanding
Never bother to ask if it is ok
to ask questions first
Might take too much time trying to grasp
the reason for the answer
Good guy wears badges like Boy Scout
earned by completing deeds and tasks
Good guy don't ask why that shirt
makes some run
Never realized that he wasn't wearing
the only badges made
That some boy scouts also learned to hunt

The best goodbye
I've ever been a part of
was packing good guy's baggage
and sending him on his way
The search for a new tenant

in this man's understanding of self
was intensive
Thank God for the caretakers
who saw fit to share
with this fractured dreamer
The only lesson that never
settled home
is the freedom in letting
cheeks wet
I've never been good
at tears falling

What I did learn is priceless
I was inspired by the number of
times I was betrayed
by good guy instincts
Confided in by partners who
survived
Survivors who didn't need to be saved
Who found understanding
in the midst of my eyes
I was challenged by fighters who
gave me books and lessons on
accountability
Pushed by men who were willing
to sit with each other in examination
of our own masculinity
Checked by soothsayers who had
seen where ignorance would lead me
Supported by a defiant band of clumsy
who were finding out how to stumble
but not fall
We had been learning to walk a certain
way for so long
The steps were unfamiliar but liberating

Each experience makes my heart full
Sobbing seems like thank you sometimes
I guess I know the reason I feel I've never
shown enough gratitude
I've just never been good at tears falling

Good guy sends me postcards
and texts saying he wants to come home
I tell him no
I've seen too much
I ain't the same man no more

I remember leaving a workshop
after talking to a group of young men
feeling heavy
I remember telling
the organizers that brought us
that there was so much work to do
What a crippling feeling it is
to do all that you know how to do
but still worrying
To fear that an angel's fall at night
could lead to a devilish dawn
I remember stopping on the side
of the road on the way home
because what wasn't being said
was deafening
I couldn't get out the car
fast enough
I remember
the comrade
who held me up
The brother who loved me
Band-Aid enough to make it home

I remember the tears

The years doing workshops with men
The programs developed
The organizations worked with
The activists I have been trained by
The survivors I have stood by
The conversations
The broken
The determined
The death threats
The resilience
The everyday reflection
The camaraderie
The betrayals
The challenges
The dismissals
The reiterations
The struggle

The beauty of healing
The burden of sustainability
The necessity of the work

The realization that silence
means that nobody ever
considers that you can
hear them
see them

I promise
The tears are never too far away

I read a comment online today
I wanted to go numb

I couldn't
I wanted to break things
but demolition is too familiar of a fancy
I wanted to cry
but I've never been good at falling tears

The water has welled in my chest
One day I will see monsoon
Or one day
I will vomit tidal waves

Burn

He is thinking of their faces
The bright-eyed hope
of students who have come to this institution
to claim their place amongst tomorrow's talented tenth
Choosing a place whose history is black
Its origin white collared
A rusting carousel
full of beautiful memories
but marred by inadequate maintenance
Their future is in his hands
What is he to do?

There is a riot inside him he is trying to calm
Excuses in full gear called to action
Tear gas and emotional shields
look like smoke and mirrors
Ask him if he is ok
Responses sound slanted like Fox News reporting
He does not want this rebellion
It took too much work to build this empire
Bribed his better judgment to look the other way
Blackmailed his optimism with past indiscretions

Isn't it amazing the things our forefathers teach us?
They say imitation is the highest form of flattery
But tradition is like a promise ring
It is used to define the present
Intended to encourage you
towards a what you want in the future
But often gets misunderstood
without the proper context

He is a scarecrow trying to protect a field of dreams
Stuck in a sticky situation
Can't keep the crows from cackling
Is treated like he doesn't have the brains
to make things right
He hangs on hoping lady luck strolls his way
She doesn't need ruby slippers
Just a strategic plan,
a dogged sense of service,
and a map to a wizard's wealth of knowledge

He has a title that is more novel than authority
Is tired of spending his days at this crossroads
where the road less traveled
is an innovative exit strategy
The road more paved is just covering up the dirt
He feels like his potential is shelved
His story hard bound
The reviews are Machiavellian

Imagine sitting in your office on a college campus
established to educate freed slaves
wondering how you got talked into tying the slipknot
on this old tire hung from a good ole boys' oak tree
Would you feel bad to know they are swinging by choice now?
That you are just making it look fun
Recycling the business model someone has no use for anymore

There are letters after his name
He got them so he'd have something to fall back on
He wanted to make a change
A difference
Found out it's different

when no one knows how to manage the change
Tries to understand silver-tongued administrators
Two-faced coins
who've lost their sense of self
Can't be trusted to stand for anything
No matter what side they choose
it's the same ignorance
He knows he can only take it at face value

There is a conscience who wants to be his pen pal
Knows he has lost touch with the right words
It sent him a self-addressed stamped envelope
so that when he finally opens his eyes
to what's going on
he can just read the truth in his soul

The instructions are clear
Write a Dear John letter to antiquated elitism
Tell them that narcissistic pragmatism
means you have to do the right thing
Not just for the kids, but for yourself
Let them know that you will not speak ill of them
You will speak to the ill they've done
You will speak to the illness they've let overrun them
There is a seething sickness here

Hold a meeting
Invite the students to the quad
Pour libation for scholars, revolutionaries,
and abolitionists with cafeteria punch
Ask for the ancestors to guide you
Light a match
Tell them that hotheaded behavior
only leads to burn out and burned bridges
Light a candle

Tell them the wick is their faith
Their education is the wax
Bind them together
The flame has a better chance at lasting
Blow it out
Remind them that a proud chest full of hot air
will only lead to dark times
Hug each one
They will know why soon enough

Go back to your office
Pack
Cry like you've never done before
Know that this is what freedom feels like
Pray for strength
Call your family and tell them you love them
The door closing gives this novel
an appropriate ending
Do not look back
Look forward
The sequel will be so much better
Then cry some more
as you shut the door of your car

Simple Complexities

3 days before the sun cursed God,
a lightning bug made love to a hurricane
beneath a rose bush.
They say the devil poked a hole in a star
and 9 months later
that bug gave birth to a tempest.
When that anomaly crowned
king of ongoing despair,
Mother Nature wet nursed it prophecy.
In celebration,
Thunder snuck into a waterfall
and stole the courage out of a larynx
hidden by ruby faced cherubim.
I haven't been able to cry over my own pain since.

At least that was the story I was committed to telling.

There is an anecdote for every falter.
a metaphor for ever aberration,
and a million ways to pretend you're not broken.
It is an eloquent show.
Like your heart hanging
from your Boabab Tree of a voice box.
Tongue branched.
Hollow inside.
Your love, compassion, and understanding
black and blue picnicked
for the white noise of your insecurities
to gawk at and laugh.
Oh, you thought joy was welcome here?

I've been begging to fall apart
for some time now.

The devil is in the duct tape.
Damn strong it is.
I've hated purpose
for the greying it does so often
when I want my angst to be
so black and white.
For sticking to the point
That there is work to do.
Heaven realized I learnt the trick
to super glue.
Nail polish removal at midnight
had me in the arms of indulgence
until it scratched me back
free from my atlas of a burden.
So, I was given adhesive instead of wings,
a pen instead of a halo.

This is the parable of a sphinx
riddled with reasons and rationales.
Searching for a gypsy
who can see tomorrow.
One who can show me an answer
in the midst of 2 onyx stones in dirt
and a redwood treasure chest of pearls.

This is the chapter and verse
of a man staffed to lead.
Wishing for a mountain peak
where I can converse
with a burning sage
and leave enlightened.
Because a Moses running errands
for a people who could care less
about the seas he had to split
to get here,

will never find peace
in people's expectations.
He'll just end up praying
day and night
to escape the golden
they have made their perceptions,
absent of any real understanding
of the work it takes to
make promise tangible.

I have shown people the glory
of a gracious gift
expecting the reward of reciprocity.
Instead, I'm left with a reputation
for being a glorious tourist attraction.

They say poems are where poets
store the artifacts of their brokenness.
So somewhere in this one
is a map that details
an adventure of understanding.
Look carefully and
you'll find revelations,
hidden meanings,
and clues.
There are cries for help
and affirmations that I'm gone be ok.
There are mirrors and flame throwers.
Coloring books and
unfinished suicide notes.
Altar calls and blasphemy.
There are Dear John letters
written to the hurt
I left behind long ago.
Birthday cards for the pain

I'll know too soon.
There are fortunes told,
promises unkept,
endings unwritten,
and doors dead bolted shut.

But there is joy.
Yes, there is joy.
A self-determined dedication
to the simple, but complex
amalgamation of magnificent
God made me.
Every night is an affirmation.
Every morning is an opportunity.
Every day breathing is a living
testimony to the reverie of resilience.

See, THAT…
that is the story I'm committed to telling.

Miracle Whip: A Villainous Villanelle

Miracle Whip is polarizing
Undeterred by contrasting perceptions
The aim is to rally its base

Moderates vary in their condiments
Revolutionaries make peanut butter and jelly sandwiches
See Miracle Whip is polarizing

They say po' folks beg for cheese in blocs
Instead of working for white bread
The aim is to rally its base

Ketchup goes best with chalk outlines
Mayonnaise is all liberalism and no fight
But Miracle Whip is polarizing

Bipartisan delis seek extravagant expansion
Say menus should be geopolitical
The aim is to rally its base

Privilege packaged all red, white, and blue
Butter knives legislated, privatized, or militarized
Miracle Whip is polarizing
Its aim is to rally its base

Wilted Flowers (for lost young lives)

My grandmother loved to tell people
about the features
she credited to the Cherokee
in her lineage
and not my father
Learnt me that the legacy
is more important than those
responsible

When the next young black tomorrow
is laid in a casket
What features will be claimed
Will the streets
activists
newspapers
claim that the legacy
is more important
than those responsible

Martyrdom has become
the new puberty
Adolescence is a ticking time bomb
seen as black terrorism
Uniformed response
is deemed fatal heroism
by jury boxes with no tongue
and no backbone

Don't hold toy guns baby boy
Don't hold a belief that arrival
will mean order baby girl
Don't move
Don't breath

Don't hope
Don't be
Contractions are abbreviated life spans
delivered by reapers
who relish
for moments to touch darkness
and manipulate it quiet

Since when were siblings suppose to
say goodbye to little brother
making pilgrimage to pearly gates
in their arms
Since when are we supposed to
get used to
flowers bedded in asphalt
becoming pollinated
by the bumble bee of gunshots

There is reason
to attack the present from all sides
until the future submits to our will
The past is filled with premature obituaries
Respectability is an improper eulogy
Ain't no need to sanitize our culture
They been wiping our blood off of concrete
The smell of bleach
is the new mistress to the dawn's sun
White out used to be the appropriate
tool to erase the presence of black ink
Now white media
is the preferred tool to negate the
humanity of black names
This here be a call for an organized
and strategic awakening

Oppression
is a brown thumbed gardener
tending to communities disregarded
by the city's fungal sense
of fiduciary responsibility
Shock transplanted in media outlets
Flowers cut down
before their purpose sees fruition
Concern waterlogging
the shoulders of blossoming buds
gathered in a protective motherly embrace
Too little light shined
on predatory or prejudiced
practices

There is no beautiful planned
for these blessing to flourish and grow
The flowers
The flowers
They wilt

Body Language

There was a trial last night
Black angst took the stand
It pledged an oath on a bible
A symbol that truths
become more pertinent in red
Sorta like blood amidst a crime scene
Our only forgotten sons

See angst was there to tell the whole truth
and nothing but the truth
so help a bullet riddled midnight
on it's way to God

This court of opinion
is oh so Machiavellian
It's all pretty play pretend
Privilege dressed
in black robed pretense
Jury box filled with cognitive dissonance,
common bigotry,
and misguided belief in a blue walled ignorance
Uniformed paradoxes with surgeon like God
complexes
and visions of black bodies as cancer
to be aggressively treated
and removed

Black bodies swinging in southern trees
gasped last rites before going home
Black bodies walking city blocks
speak in a resilient vernacular
Prosecution say it sound so criminal
Like probable cause

Defense say ain't nobody ever
really wanted to listen to the body language

Prosecution say stance was aggressive
Hands say I showed my palms
Thought the flushed pink there
might mirror
the panicked hatred facing them
Can't turn, might seem like welcoming
Like ground control for flying rounds
looking to land on dark tarmacs
Can't close, might seem like resistance
Like fight back
Like justified kill

Prosecution say movement seemed shady
Feet just wanted to be mo careful
They have been blamed
for the toppling oaks before
Feet say they stood still
Feet say 10 toes down
better than 10 toes up
Feet say they felt the earth giggle with glee
at the promise of dinner

Newspapers say there was a prior record
Mouths speak words like good,
determined, promising
Tell tales of youthfulness
Sing sad songs
Teeth wave goodbye
as they run from baton against jaw
Mouth cry red tears for teeth lost
City cries red tears for youth lost

Gun said on your knees
Knees kiss earth in prayer
Scream when ripped from the asphalt embrace
Eyes watch night cloaked death
strike again and again
Then eyes close in self-preservation
Skin cracks
Head craters
Levees break
Red floods cities of hope and humanity

Prosecution says nothing was done wrong
Work means job to do
Clock ticks too precious for mercy
Questions are for courtrooms
not life or death situations
Judges get to take the black off
When it no longer suits them
12 still arguing the times
Respectability and misrepresentation
Thugs and criminality
Duty and service
Training and in the blink of an eye
Post racial and 400-year burdens
Glory and demonization
Martyrdom and marginalization
Defense can never rest
Defense can never rest
Defense can never rest

Blues for Midnight

Bullets are not shooting stars
Wishes and closed eyes
have been hand in hand
since our youth
So justice stays blind to
imperialism's wishes that we would go away
or stay…in our place
While society stays blindfolded by
a belief that things have actually changed

So I sing a blues for midnight
Because we are still afraid of the dark
Still caught in the horror of it all
Ask Alfred Hitchcock
if he knew they shoot shadows
Sending light piecing into them
until red signals them to stop

We lose our young at the end of rainbows
Our colored girls when it's enuf
Our young men before they can taste them
Or wash them down with a brisk sense of satisfaction
What you want with them colors black girl
You can't have them colors black boy
You might think you as beautiful
Might think you equal
Put them colors down African child
or we'll make the Nile run
from your momma's eyes

It is said that
Black is the absence of light
Calm collectivity

Mama said be in
by the time the streetlights came on
because fallen angels with halogen halos
do the devil's work
Making it easier for constellations
to be drawn across black skin

I sing a blues for midnight
Because black holes start
with collapsing stars
Even the universe knows the fate of melanin hued skin
Comet cannot cleanse dark spots
Mr. Clean is not a skinhead
We are not monsters
Bullets are not shooting stars

I sing a blues for midnight
Dancing to the melody as I march
Writing fight chants on the wind with my tongue
Listen to the airwaves
Radio Free Dixie
Nod your head to the tune
It's a party
A revolutionary party
Didn't freedom fighters teach us that
it's our civil right to resist
They knew we might not see the dawn's sun
unless we learned how to protect the night ourselves
Past the tears falling like rain
Past the pain
Chalk outlines
and faulty media reporting

Whenever a black life is lost
I sing a blues

Call it midnight
Their families left in mourning
Their loved one will never see morning
Because somebody afraid of the dark we covered in
Afraid of ravens walking
upon a midnight dreary
Fearing it as demon
Seeing them as birds of prey
To Kill a Mockingbird
all you need is the right excuse
and the right appearance

I got "Trouble in Mind" Nina
I asked Thelonious
What happens "Round Midnight"
He say piano lessons taught him
to know the black keys
by the white ones they were surrounded by
When midnight melodies
become funeral processionals
We remember black life
by the white one they were killed by

Ma Rainey taught us how to go on record
stand for something
Momma knows best
William Henry Lane showed us
how they really feel about black faces
when he stepped on those minstrel show stages
So I need us to learn to sing a blues for midnight
A revolutionary reverie
that inspires a radical resistance
Use our voice and presence
from the classroom to the boardroom
Senate chambers to town hall

Make "Small Talk at 125th and Lennox"
and "Across 110th Street"
Remember them "88 Seconds in Greensboro"

Sing a blues for midnight
Teach it to your brother and sisters
Sons and daughters
Until the melody haunts like a guilty conscience
Because bullets are not shooting stars
The next time they invade the night sky
I might not make it home

Sciaphobia

Sciaphobia is a fear of shadows
said to arise from a combination of external events
and internal predispositions
often traced to a triggering event,
usually a traumatic experience at a young age
Symptoms vary depending on a person's level of fear
They can include extreme anxiety, dread
and anything associated with panic
such as shortness of breath, irregular heartbeat,
sweating, nausea,
gunshots, cover-ups, defamation, tire irons,
vehicular homicide, racial profiling, and righteous
indignation

Sciaphobia is often introduced by someone
who has their own personal fear of shadows.
It can be generational, the result of observed behavior
Propagandized and used for power positioning
Litigated and used to fill prison cells
Legislated and used to build soapboxes
on the backs of the working class
Mansions on the shoulders of middle class idealism

It is said that the fear goes back to anxiety
related to the identity of the source of the shadow
Is it what lurks beyond the light of the torch
Lady Liberty holds
A worry about the oppressed
you have turned your back on
growing more fed up over your shoulder
The trauma from knowing that even after emancipation
dark bodies were beaten
lynched and killed with no regard

Paranoia over those you've made hate you?
Monsters manufactured through media, rhetoric
and militarized action
Bombs dropped cast shadows off into the hills
Don't try to fool us by calling them terrorists or
insurgents

America,
do you realize you are afraid of shadows

You see them in the parts of town you try to forget
But hoods filled with dark skin are not dangerous
Do not be fooled
I know who really made hoods infamous
Setting fire fueled by prejudice
to anywhere darkness gathered
Casting shadows into libraries and documentaries
while keeping a post racial lamp lit on rundown rhetoric
But Tom Bodette taught us that a light left on
is a cheap trick

The closet has always been a dark place
and we have been taught to fear what lurks in the dark
But isn't that where we keep what covers us?
When did it become a place where we hide
what we want to cover up?
Dear conservative Christian fundamentalists
The divine light you hold so piously to
cast the shadows you place in closets
I'm not talking about the same sex couples
you ran to the polls to deny
by passing Amendment One
The indiscretions you don't want anyone
to be aware of
Be honest about why you don't want the door open

You're even more afraid of what else might escape

Tell me
have you ever tried shadowboxing
Deryl Dedmond and his boys did
Then sent a F250 spiraling into James Anderson
like a meteor into an abysmal dark
Sciaphobia is often introduced by someone
who has their own personal fear of shadows
A Black Nissan plant worker
was run over by a Ford truck
Damn Dedmond and his boys learned
American privileged pride real well

Map me a dead butterfly's path home
and I'll show you the ignorance of someone
that knows nothing beautiful
Covering the color of a butterfly's wings
doesn't mean it's ok to swat at it like a fly
Her head covered in tradition and faith
I guess someone thought
she wasn't open minded enough
Shaima Alawadi was wearing a hijab
They saw a shadow
Took a tire iron and made it into a shroud
Folks searched the news
Hoping that it was repressive patriarchy
and not oppressive bigotry that took her life
What person wishes for one over the other
to ease their guilty conscious

America,
do you realize you're afraid of shadows

Safe

We were standing outside the venue
Warriors celebrating in reverie
after a night of competition
A communion of respect and rebellion
Poets amassed in camaraderie
The city could feel the movement in motion
I guess it thought the stage wasn't bright enough
Figured we needed some flashing lights

To the police officer who said my friend
was in the best hands he could be in
Could you hear the moon laugh at your arrogance?
Did you feel the night gasp at the assertion?
I admire the magician in your sense of authority
but I am not impressed by the illusion

Have you not realized
that your badge has become a funhouse mirror?
My value distorted in your presence
Uniform as crippling as the legend of Medusa's glare
Too often we find ourselves crumbling in your grasp
Scattered like dust across the flat line of the news

Your words felt like syndicated soap opera
The drama of a relationship gone so wrong
We argue
You call your friends
6 patrol cars, 1 paddy wagon
I wonder why I ever trusted you
You tell me you're what's best for me
I say I don't need you
You say you won't let me go
Then I have to call my friends collect

to come get me
It is such a rancid routine

Maybe
You realized you were talking to a black man
Knew that safety is usually the justification
for you showing up and handcuffing me instead
Thought I'd feel an ironic sense of relief
that it was a white man you held
Your tone was all assumption and probable pause
Cause and effect in your hand inching to waist
I was embarrassed my feet moved
before my mouth asked questions
I am sure you were confident
I'd understand your body language

In the moments as black poets dispersed
Did you chuckle childlike at the irony
of oil flooding the streets
Rich in value, crude
Was the British Petroleum in your posture
supposed to be a privileged inside joke?
10 white men surrounding the
1 white boy
detained on the hood of a cruiser
Was his matching skin tone not good ole boy enough?
Did he seem too comfortable amongst the dark?
Were you keeping him
or trying to save him?
Remind him of his place
Learn him
that southern moons don't blend into the night sky

How dare you?
We were just poets gathered outside a venue

What law were we breaking?
Was the freedom too disturbing?
Was the joy too threatening?
Did you mistake the YouTube videos and flyers
for police blotters and wanted posters?

Please pardon my concern
I've heard you have a voracious appetite
That a date with you
is often a bail bondage experience
Something about chokeholds,
tasers, and beatings
Gunshots searing flesh like cigarette burns
In the wrong house
Over what was thought to be a weapon
In the back of patrol cars
A sadomasochistic impulse too often reported justified
An orgy of insatiable lust
Got me searching for safe words
like rights, innocence, lawyer, pineapples

To the ignorance uniformed in growing frustration
I'm sorry we didn't move fast enough
Didn't feel comforted by your assertion
Worried what would happen
when all the eyes and smart phones left the scene
See I don't want to pen no memorials
I don't want to
shed no tears over scratched out lines
and torn pages tossed away
by a vicious editor
who prefers journals shackle bound
One who salivates
at handcuff spiraled notebooks

So you can usher us away with your arrogant coddling
But let me assure you
We will stay close enough
that we can easily double back
to claim what is ours and not yours
What we protect and serve
See Officer
Ours is an undeniable truth
That the safest place for him to ever be
is with us

Spike Lee

on a grey clouded night in December
God looked down
the weight of ubiquity furrowing his brow
turned to Gabriel
and with the whimsy of a
butterfly's summer flight pattern
wrote two words across the heavens
"Spike Lee"
thunder bellowed
lightning struck
and the plight of black America
began to reel below them

academic institutions felt the ripple across campus
the collective yawn of a million black faces
awakening from the daze
feels like damn breaking
flood of tears coming
no recourse to stop it
from the office of admissions
to the class room
narrow minded elitism
dances like final curtain call
self determination
feels like radical transformation
like self awareness
and diasporic understanding

respectability politics abound
what to do, what to do?
conservative bourgeois disillusionment
wants a close up
do the right thing

scream it across airwaves, across radios
protect the middle class
they deserve a slice
black terror and state served ineptitude
will ruin our capital salvation

no black man in the white house
will make this mo betta
no black boy walking down the street
no questions asked of unnecessary stop
will make it mo better
no black prosecuting attorney
no black officials
no organizing
be rose lensed negroes
trusting
mo betta blues
wearing badges and hate
like pride
to protect and serve you

damn white privilege look sexy
damn while supremacy got a whole lotta back
but concrete jungles and country porches
ain't fit for bunnies and monkeys
we prefer you lonely in America

X marks the spot where bullet holes
have become the autobiography
for young black boys
a white draped pilgrimage to a morgue
a black powerful funeral procession
an assassinated future
a pain written in the depths of our angst
a loss we still can't make peace with

ask Crooklyn about a heavy-handed Rudy
New Jersey can tell you the jury"s still out
on Ras Baraka's driving force
we clocking St. Louis, Oakland, Baltimore
folks getting on buses
they gone make it Charleston, Sanford, Charlotte
we gone scream these tales from the hood
cuz what we can tell from the hood
is you afraid to share this new age
burning crosses and churches
holding on to the flag of a battle long lost
it will serve you well when you lose again

we must combat our misguided
she got to have it mentality
dial back our girl 6 desires
we will not let patriarchy overwhelm us
she hate me is a rhetoric
best considered passing strange
don't believe it
this here be a sucker free city

4 little girls
all the invisible children
we will say her name
we will say their names
we will remember that a black life lost
is a hell we don't want purgatory in

see, the devil got game
a freakish desire for black pain
sadomasochistic impulse
politicians got excuses

dangle puppets like
we supposed to believe
he the best man for the job
we find it comedy
how privilege stages our kings
to topple later in scandal
do any of them cry when they realize
they have been bamboozled?

my God
this undisputed truth
it's been there all along
Gabriel says
marveling at how the father
plays great reveal with destiny
how genius is just prophecy
yet to be recognized

then with the beaming bright
of a celestial body in his smile
God continues to write
"has yet to grasp
what I am doing with him"
it was then Gabriel realized
that as redemption
is da sweet blood of Jesus
so is ego
da bitter aftertaste of ignorance
but Lord knows
he means well
he means well

Everything Worth Fighting For

There is a joy that comes with seeing
groups of children playing
in an open field
A twinge in your gut that comes
when passing a sun kissed testimony
in tattered clothes
holding court on a corner
A smile that forms
when a phone call affirms
that hard work has placed
another snapshot of black excellence
where the world can see
An affirming head nod
that says that
in a room of obstacles and expectation
we belong here

There is the pride
that beams at youthful recital
Cheers that accompany
athletic achievement
A hug that starter pistols
the next glorious gathering
of friends
Laughter that chronicles
The best of times
Tears that fall
During the worst times

These are the moments
that let us know that there is
so much worth fighting for

I know a cadre of will
talking bout toppling institutions
and dismantling systems
of oppression
in the back room of a church
2 prayers from a liquor house
Down the street
from a school named after an optimist
Around the corner
from a complex
considered an eyesore
with low property values
that has birthed more blessings
than bastards
These dedicated rebels
are planning demonstration
Coordinating childcare
Identifying roles and tasks
Building capacity with a passion unmatched
Their discussions are a joyful noise

These are the visionaries
who know that there is
so much worth fighting for

See there is promise
wrestling with purpose
in a classroom
during the late hour
They are inspired by the tales
of ancestors before
Searching for victory after
They came with questions
and are leaving

with a focused strategy
This is where developing minds
seek greater understanding
past professors and syllabi
Together
Here
careers and families
are distant actualizations
of a tuition paid journey
Today
Today is where they sharpen
their skills at crafting
a wonderfully sculpted
happy ending
Tomorrow
They will march and demand
Pushing administration
to consider that dorm rooms
are not margins
That the blueprints of their future
should have etchings
from their own hands

They are everything worth fighting for

There are neighborhoods to reclaim
Lost lives to honor with resilience
Names to say
Legacies to build
Ancestors to invoke
Text to review
Positions to be held
Stories to be told
Lessons to be learned
Insight to be passed

Programs to be developed
Work to be done

My God
Don't you feel it?
Can't you see it?

There is truth clotheslined
along the horizon
Hung by angels
who want us to see
what this world is meant to be
There
drying by the light of the sun
is woven inspiration
covered in the tears
of those who left
before the battle was won

Sitting in your house right now
is a mirror
with an honest tongue
and a glimmer in its eye
Waiting to have a
Heart-to-heart conversation
with you
It has a message to deliver
in familiar clarity
A promise to make
A revelation to share
A desire to let you know
that if you take a look there
that it can show you
everything worth fighting for

Epilogue

There have been so many amazing influences in how activism and organizing fit into my life. There is no way I can list them all, but I can take a moment to acknowledge that I have had the honor of working with, learning with, growing with, organizing with and fighting with some of the most incredible people, thinkers, revolutionaries.

Thank You

No, really...THANK YOU

I am a Black artist. A choice I have made with the full understanding of the legacy, the struggle, and the responsibility the designation carries. It is in recognition of the Black artists before me that I strive to do the best work I can.

I am a dreamer. I am a dreamer who will never stop looking deeper, reaching further, and thinking broadly. I am a dreamer who believes that the visions I hold will continue to push me forward.

I am a creative.

I am a scholar.

I am. We are.

We will

Win

www.ingramcontent.com/pod-product-compliance
Lightning Source LLC
Chambersburg PA
CBHW071252070526
44583CB00017B/2431